When it was my turn to hit the pillow, out of nowhere I found myself swinging the bat and striking the pillow with such force and passion. The intensity must have come from something inside me that needed to be released. Something was being brought to the surface. Something from my past. My unresolved issues. I felt emotions beyond words. Pain, fear, terror, and panic overwhelmed me. I saw and felt things from my past that left me unresponsive, unable to speak, as if in a shadow of death.

After hitting and hitting the pillow, I fell to the floor sobbing. It was a cry so deep, a cry so profoundly forbidden, that I lay alone with the memories that I had kept hidden, never wanting to awaken them. I just lay there on the cold, forsaken floor, not wanting anyone to touch or assist me in any way. I wanted to be alone. I wanted to get back to the land of forgetting.

Remembering and Forgetting

a spiritual journey

Lin Day

Atkins & Greenspan Publishing

Copyrighted Material
Remembering and Forgetting: *a spiritual journey*
Copyright © 2018 by Lin Day. All Rights Reserved.

No part of this publication may be reproduced, stored in a retrieval system or transmitted, in any form or by any means — electronic, mechanical, photocopying, recording, or otherwise — without prior written permission from the publisher, except for the inclusion of brief quotations in a review.

For information about this title or to order other books and/or electronic media, contact the publisher:

Atkins & Greenspan Publishing
18530 Mack Avenue, Suite 166
Grosse Pointe Farms, MI 48236
www.atkinsgreenspan.com

ISBN:
978-1-945875-31-1 (Hardcover)
978-1-945875-32-8 (Paperback)
978-1-945875-33-5 (eBook)

Printed in the United States of America

Cover and Interior design: Van-garde Imagery

Photographs used with permission.

Dedication

This book is dedicated to Dr. Kim Manning,
who believed in me
and my ability to become my authentic self.

In Gratitude

HOW DO YOU THANK so many people who have been instrumental in forming your life...

My sincere and heartfelt love and appreciation to everyone who has helped bring this book to life. I want to thank first and foremost my three Spiritual Guides: Myrtle my Guardian Angel, Archangel Raphael, and my Spiritual Guide Kimmy who dictated the book through Spirit as I listened and typed away. My spiritual support was unending, and Divine guidance was my true and pure counsel.

To my brothers, George Day and Eric Day, and my sister, Pat Fitch. I love them more than they will ever know.

My sincere and unending gratitude to Dr. Kim Manning who supported and believed in me that I could reach my goals and become my authentic self.

To Jeanne Salkowski, who was the first and only person I dared to let read the first few chapters of the book. Jeanne warmheartedly encouraged me to continue writing. Without her ongoing support and reassurance, I'm not sure I would have continued.

To Joyce Rupp, my beloved friend whom I have had the privilege of sharing my life with for the past 24 years; she shared her home, her family, and friends with me in the best of times and the most heartbreaking of times. She has been a true champion throughout all these years.

To Dee Acho who called and suggested I go to the Detroit Library knowing my interest in writing a book.

To my wonderful co-workers from Macomb County Mental Health whom I had the pleasure of working with the past 18 years. Especially Tammy Kerchkof, who was always there for me, my office buddy and dearest friend. Debbie Schmidt, who encouraged me to see a hypnotherapist in the first place. A true and loyal friend, Janet Fulkins, who always brightened my day by sharing pictures of her grandchildren, a wonderful and dear friend.

To Marianne Frazho who always makes me laugh until it hurts, a true friend who has always been there for me.

To my dearest and longest friends Grace and George Seroka, who have always been there throughout all these years, and all the years to come.

I want to thank Elizabeth Atkins and Catherine Greenspan, my editors and publisher for their enthusiasm and excitement with each and every contact whether by e-mail or text. Elizabeth's kindness and support were comforting and reassuring, always encouraging. Never once did I feel discouraged to continue writing. With Catherine, I experienced the same continued support. These two ladies are so fantastic and I am so blessed that Spirit chose these two to play such a major role in having my book come to be.

I don't want anyone to feel left out, so please know that everyone in my life whether mentioned or not is truly appreciated and loved by me.

Love your beautiful selves as I do,

Lin

Contents

Dedication v

In Gratitude vii

Foreword by Dr. Kim Manning xi

Chapter 1 1

Chapter 2 7

Chapter 3 9

Chapter 4 13

Chapter 5 17

Chapter 6 23

Chapter 7 29

Chapter 8 33

Chapter 9 39

Chapter 10 43

Chapter 11 49

Chapter 12 55

Chapter 13 59

Chapter 14 65

Chapter 15 69

Chapter 16 75

Epilogue 83

About Lin Day 85

Foreword

My chosen profession as a Medical Hypnotherapist is so satisfying and rewarding that in order to truly understand it, you'd have to experience it yourself, either from a personal perspective or from the perspective of my clients.

Lin Day's story is just an example to this statement. I met Lin in my office in September of 2017. Like so many others, she had a goal in mind… Lin said she wanted to lose weight, approximately 70 pounds, and she wanted to reconnect with her true spiritual being. When discussing Lin's history, it was not so remarkable or overly complicated, but it was very interesting … and the progression of her life choices made for an easy roadmap to follow lending insight to her presenting concerns. I found Lin to be very articulate and selfless as well as quite intuitive. During our initial discussion this day, Lin shared that she had sought out many therapists and therapies but still had a block of some sort. Lin made it known that she was ready to live again, wanted control over her life, and was willing to do whatever was necessary in order to reach her goals.

Lin had been in a convent for some years before she was employed as a licensed social worker where she worked with the mentally challenged population for many years before retiring. In the interim, Lin was a recipient of many therapy sessions and therapeutic modalities, so it's accurate to say that Lin was no stranger to the value of self-help and healing. Lin had successfully helped many suffering individuals in her lifetime but was still unable to help herself, even after seeking help and training from some of the most renowned leaders in the field. This is what identifies Lin to so many other self-seekers in our community out there. We can and so often do, help others, but when it comes to self, we just can't get there for some reason or other. Lin recognized that she could identify that something was not quite right and that her inner self was crying out while her outer self was struggling but unable to fully be free from "it" — whatever "it" was. The issues that Lin presented with were the symptoms to a deeper upset and only getting to the root of the cause was going to make any permanent change. Lin intuitively knew this and therefore never gave up the search.

As I often say, the reward is the results… and there is no greater reward than the one I experience when a client of mine makes a breakthrough and is fully released from the trauma(s) of their past. And this is Lin's story, safe and free to live in the here and now, moving ever forward to her goals and life ambitions… being her true, authentic self, loving herself unconditionally, free of guilt, shame or blame and some 42-plus pounds lighter.

Lin's story will teach one a lot about the power of determination, the mind, sacrifices, and hope… This is a true story of a beautiful human being who once was trapped in her own body on a life journey looking for a way out. It is a story of selflessness, survival, courage,

a spirtual journey

and a relentless search for truth and soulfulness. This is Lin Day's story, and I'm so pleased to have met such a powerfully inspiring woman on that September day in 2017.

Kim Manning, PhD
Focused Solutions
Michigan Hypnotherapy
Bloomfield Hills, Michigan

Chapter 1

THIS IS A STORY about a life, a story you can believe is true, or one that you don't believe is true. It doesn't matter. It starts out like any ordinary story, and it is my story. I was born to an ordinary family with a mother and father. My father worked for one of the big four automotive companies, and my stay-at-home mom took care of four kids: my sister, two brothers, and me, the youngest. As I look back on my childhood, I find myself reflecting on the memories that I love the most.

My friends, family members, and colleagues know how much I love Christmas. This magical holiday is truly "the most wonderful time of the year." Bright, colorful lights. Playing in the snow. Decorating Christmas trees. Visiting my grandmas, grandpas, aunts, and uncles. And, of course, opening presents. I was about four or five years old when I realized even with all the excitement of Christmas swirling in my head, an uneasiness and discomfort gnawed the pit of my stomach.

I knew my mother was not happy even during this joyous time of year. I could tell by the way she walked and by the sound of her voice when she was in the other room. I could feel that something was going on in her mind. I so wanted her to be happy, less depressed, less anxious, less angry. Because when she was happy, I felt free to be happy, too.

Sometimes she was in a good mood. Her smile and laugh would light up the room. Her eyes would shine and be bright. She could be so childlike, being silly and teasing us kids, but those moments were rare.

I always felt that I needed to be aware of her moods and to remain watchful for any changes. I knew that her facial expressions and the tone of her voice always revealed her mood and told a story.

Most of the time, my mother seemed like other mothers, but she seemed a little more fragile, more out of control than my friends' mothers. I loved her, and as a child, I so much wanted her to be happy ALL the time.

The wonderful Christmas season set the backdrop for dramatic contrast in our home. My mother would be in the kitchen making cookies, coffee cakes, homemade bread, and whatever else mothers do to make a merry Christmas for their families.

But all of a sudden, she would stop, rush to where I was playing with my sister and brothers.

"You're being too loud!" she'd yell, looking furious. "Stop roughhousing!"

We were just being kids; we hadn't done anything wrong. But the way she shouted and glared at us made me feel that I was bad, and that I had done something very wrong. This left me feeling heartbroken and sad. These sentiments felt even worse during the fun of the holiday season. But no matter what, I still found Christmas wonderful, and still do to this day, even if some of the magic of that childhood belief is gone.

Being the youngest member of the family brought its ups and downs. Before I was born, as the story goes, my sister and brothers argued over what sex I was going to be. My brothers wanted a cowboy brother and my sister wanted a cowgirl sister. My sister won! My mother had all four of us kids within five-and-a-half years. My sister was about five-and-a-half years old, my oldest brother was four, and the brother before me was three years older than me. Somewhere in that deep subconscious of my young mind was a feeling that I wasn't wanted, that my mother already had too much on her plate and didn't need another child. That thought echoed somewhere in my memory for as long as I can remember, even to this day.

I don't have much of a memory of the first five or six years of my life until I started to remember, and I will tell you more about that later. It seems my life was a series of remembering and forgetting, thus the name of the book. I am getting off track here, so allow me to continue.

School

I didn't like school. I felt stupid and embarrassed because I stuttered. I went to Catholic school until the eighth grade, and unlike many stories I've heard from other people, I loved the nuns. I felt comforted and accepted by them.

You see, my mother suffered from mental illness (if you hadn't already guessed that). She was angry, upset, or depressed most of the time, and the nuns somehow felt like a shield from all that. I felt safe with the nuns; I didn't always feel safe at home. I loved being at school, even though I wasn't good at school work.

In my Catholic school, the desks were arranged in rows with the smartest kids in the front, and the dumbest in the back. You guessed it, I was in the last row, but not in the last seat, thank God. I was well-liked by my peers; they didn't treat me like the dumb kid I thought I was. The kids in my class liked me, and I liked them. I felt accepted. I was always making jokes and playing around. My friends could count on me being there for them when they needed me. I was not the smartest kid in the class, nor was I the dumbest.

 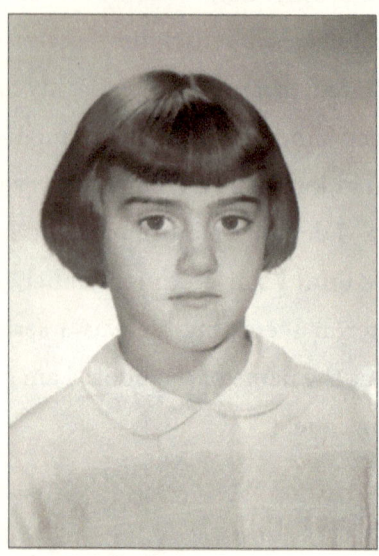

Photographs of me as a child.

It wasn't until high school that I started getting better grades. It was my English teacher who helped me feel smart for the first time in my educational life. She told me I was a good thinker, and I wrote a good paper. From that time on, I did better in school. I was never the kid who got all A's; I was happy to get C's and D's. However, after I got that first A in Miss Ann's English class, I did better in school.

High school was filled with flirting with good-looking boys, going to dances, making out under the bleachers at football games, and hanging out with friends. I always enjoyed being with my friends and singing in some of the garage bands. Rock bands were big in the late sixties. I enjoyed high school, but was looking forward to getting out and graduating.

It was in high school, however, that I started to think of my faith more personally. I didn't go to Catholic high school, but I went to catechism classes on Monday nights, where I met up with many of my grade-school friends who also didn't go on to Catholic high school. Growing up in the sixties was the best; we questioned everything and wanted to change the world for the better.

We thought our parents didn't know anything about what was *really* important. We wanted things to change, to see life differently, more honestly and truthfully, but we didn't have any idea how to do it. But in those catechism classes, we talked about making God more real and not some scary guy who was out to judge and punish us.

We started a youth group at our church where we discussed how Jesus was a man who taught love and acceptance. The sixties were all about love and peace.

I remember as a child looking through the screen of my bedroom window and seeing the reflection of a cross. God was someone who not only watched over me to protect me but was one who would also punish me. My mother always told me that if I did something wrong and she didn't find out about it, God would see me and would punish me. So, if I fell off my bike or skinned my knee, I knew it was God punishing me for something I did wrong. That was not the God I wanted to know.

We girls from that catechism class decided to go on retreat. Most of us knew each other from grade school. None of us were aware of it at the time, but it was a stakeout to see if any of us girls were nun material or who might be thinking of religious life. I don't think any of us were, and I, in no way, was thinking about being a nun. I was too boy crazy and was considered the class clown. I had no discipline and was not known for obeying the rules, but by the end of the retreat I felt something stirring in me: curiosity or inquisitiveness of what it would be like to be a nun. Remember, I always felt accepted and safe with the nuns in grade school.

I talked to one of the nuns privately on the retreat about my growing feelings, and wondered if just maybe I was being "called." I had a chance to talk with Sister Mary Ann, who wasn't much older than me. She willingly shared how and when she knew she had a calling for religious life. She told me that she, too, was confused at the beginning about religious life, but it became clearer as time went on. Sister Mary Ann and I became good friends that weekend.

I would be graduating in June and still didn't know if I had a calling or not. I spoke with Sister Mary Ann several times during my senior year. But since I still wasn't sure what I wanted to do with my life, Sister Mary Ann suggested I work at the children's orphanage run by the Sisters of Divine Love after I graduated. She said the experience of working at the orphanage would give me a better understanding and knowledge of religious life.

I started working at the orphanage the week after I graduated. My dad wasn't too happy with me leaving home, because he believed that a girl never left home until she was married. But, we're talking about me here now, and being a little rebellious and defiant was in my blood.

I didn't want to tell my parents I was thinking of religious life; I guess because I didn't think they would believe me. No one would; I definitely was not the nun type.

Chapter 2

My life at the orphanage was full of experiences I will never forget, nor would I ever want to. I lived on campus with about six other girls around my age who also worked at the orphanage. We lived on campus because we worked split shifts and rent was cheap. None of the other girls that I knew of were thinking of religious life, and I kept my secret to myself. We worked in the morning starting at 7:00 a.m. for about three hours while the sisters went to Mass and ate breakfast. We got the children up, dressed, fed, and ready for the day until the sisters came to relieve us. We returned and worked again from 3:00 p.m. until 8:00 p.m.

Many times, after the end of my evening shift, Sister Mary Ann and I would spend time talking about religious life and life in general. Our talks often lasted until late in the evening. The orphanage had several individual cottages, each one bearing a name that symbolized the Catholic Church or that from the order of the Sisters of Divine Love. The cottages were connected to each other inside a beautiful aesthetic building built in the early 1900s. Each cottage housed about 14 to 16 children. A sister was assigned to one cottage with one staff member during the week and with two on the weekends. I usually didn't work the weekends unless one of the other weekend staff couldn't work. The cottages were separated by age and gender: girls in one and boys in the other. The children's ages ranged from infants to 14. Bethlehem cottage was comprised of the nursery. The babies in the nursery came from a home for unwed mothers.

I was assigned to St. Michaels cottage with 16 boys who ranged from eight to 11 years old. Sister Mary Paul oversaw the cottage. She was moody, and I was a little afraid of her in the beginning. The boys were downright scared of her.

Over time I began to understand Sister Mary Paul's moods because of my experience with my mother's moods. Sister Mary Paul even became someone I looked up to and admired. She was a gentle lady who was afraid to show that side of herself. I truly came to love her. When I was not working, I took a few community college classes and hung out with some of the other girls who worked at the orphanage. I'll skip all the in-between stuff and go straight to the summer that I opened my mind and heart to a myriad of life experiences.

Chapter 3

It was the summer of 1968, Sister Mary Paul and I, with all 16 boys, were spending an overnight at the orphanage's summer camp where we'd all go swimming and fishing. At one point, Sister Mary Paul was called back to the convent and had to leave after lunch. Mike, the seminarian from Sacred Heart Seminary, was coming to relieve her. He worked with the boys on the weekends and enjoyed being with them. He volunteered to relieve Sister Mary Paul and agreed to stay overnight.

I knew Mike, and we had become good friends. I was looking forward to seeing him, and the boys were overjoyed. Having Sister Mary Paul around left us on edge, knowing we all had to be on our best behavior. Once Mike got there, we would all feel free to be ourselves and enjoy the rest of the day without the watchful eye of Sister Mary Paul.

After dinner, and after the last swim of the evening, the boys washed up and got ready for bed. No one needed a shower due to being in the water all day. We decided to have snacks that Mike and the boys made. We enjoyed them around the campfire, singing typical camp songs like *Kumbaya* and *Michael Rowed the Boat Ashore*. I even made some up myself. Yes, I played the guitar, and we all ate too many s'mores. The boys and Mike coerced me into sleeping under the stars with them in a sleeping bag by showing me the beautiful stars, the brightly lit moon, and the warmth of summer night air.

Who could say no? It was such a beautiful warm summer night. The stars filled the entire sky like little twinkling night lights.

After the boys were asleep, Mike suggested we sit on the dock near the water and talk. We sat with our toes dangling in the warm water with just a sliver of the moon bouncing off the water. We were close enough to the boys to hear them in case one of them needed us.

Mike and I enjoyed each other's company. He was a seminarian, planning on becoming a priest, while I was planning to become a nun. We talked about the church, our lives, religious life, and what changes we wanted to see the church make. It was all very innocent; we talked well into the night.

All of a sudden, while looking up at one of the most beautiful summer skies, and stars that appeared to be dancing with each other, one broke away, falling straight toward us. We looked at that sky in such amazement, disbelief, and silence for a long time. Then, out of the blue, Mike pulled me into him and kissed me. Though I'd had lots of experience kissing under the bleachers at football games, I'd never felt anything like Mike's kiss before. His kiss was like all those stars in that welcoming sky coming down and settling in my flickering heart. My heart and mind were beating fast, out of control. I was floating in a sea of emotions.

After what seemed like a long time, he pulled away. I was breathless, lost in the moment. He apologized, saying he didn't know what came over him. We were both confused and sat in silence for what seemed like an eternity, holding each other close. I couldn't stop thinking about how marvelous his kiss was. I didn't want it to stop; I wanted to kiss him again and again. I didn't seem to have control over myself or my desires. I wanted more, and this time I moved in and started kissing him. He didn't stop me. We kissed as if the gods were permitting us, free of any guilt or shame…

When I saw Mike's face that next morning, everything had changed. With the dawn of a new day, it seemed like the night before had been a dream. I could see he was deep in thought. His eyes communicated concern and confusion.

For Christ's sake, what were we thinking? He was going to become a priest and I a nun!

We didn't talk much to each other that next morning, and Sister Mary Paul showed up earlier than expected. I swear she knew something was going on. Mike and I showed no signs, we hoped, of the night before, but it weighed heavily on my heart. I spent the rest of the day in the water with the boys, watching them swim back and forth to the raft that floated several feet from the dock. Mike took some of the boys out on the boat to go fishing.

Sister Mary Paul watched from the porch of the cabin like an eagle-hawk, waiting for one of the boys to do something wrong, so she could discipline them. I just thought they were boys being boys. Sister Mary Paul saw things differently. She would suddenly call one of the boys out of the water, with me in tow. The poor boy would have to sit on the shore while I got instructed on how I needed to watch the boys more closely. It was always interesting to me that I could never see what they ever did wrong.

When it was finally time to pack up and head back to the orphanage, a part of me wanted to stay to have more time alone with Mike. Another part of me knew that was not going to happen.

The ride back on the bus was quieter than usual. The boys were very tired, and many of them fell asleep. I was quieter too; I didn't want to do anything. I wanted to be alone with my thoughts. Usually, I would play my guitar, but uncertainty and fear filled my mind and heart. I was no longer as confident of my future. What did the night before mean? Did it mean anything?

Sister Mary Paul and Mike drove back in his car. Once we were all back at the orphanage, Mike helped get the boys' things off the bus and helped them get settled in for the night.

Mike and I said goodbye without making eye contact. It was like we didn't want to see what the other was feeling. I knew we wouldn't see each other again until the following weekend, which couldn't come fast enough.

Chapter 4

MIKE WAS ON TIME for his shift; I was filling in that morning because the girl who was supposed to work called in sick. I wasn't sure if he was going to show up. Would I ever see him again?

Maybe he decided I was too much of a distraction to his becoming a priest. Once we did make eye contact, I felt awkward and strange. I didn't know how to interact with him. I was surprised how my heart raced; I felt my face getting red, my stomach full of nerves. I thought Mike looked the same, or was it something else I was seeing? I didn't know. We didn't talk to each other very much unless we had to and kept our distance. I found myself looking at him, trying to read his feelings. I wanted so much to know what he was thinking and feeling. If our eyes met, I swiftly looked away. I didn't want him to know I was watching him.

I had almost a full week to think about the weekend, what had happened, and what I was feeling. Confusion for sure, and sadness. I also felt ashamed that I was interfering with a man becoming a priest. I couldn't get the feelings and thoughts of that night out of my mind. I wanted to be kissed by him again, to feel his body next to mine, to feel our hearts beating in unison, and for the magic of that night to return. My thoughts haunted me. They were so wrong! I thought, *I should be ashamed of myself!* I wanted to go to confession but knew I couldn't. I couldn't tell anyone, not even my dearest friend and confidant, Sister Mary Ann. How could I talk to her about Mike? I had already applied for the convent. Everyone knew Mike was going to be a priest and I a nun. My whole world had turned upside down. I was no longer sure of my future. How could this have happened?

I was about to leave the cottage because the other staff came in to take my place. The nuns didn't like to pay overtime, and I had already put in a full week of work. I was leaving when Mike came running up to me.

Winded and out of breath, he asked, "Can I see you after I get off work?"

I wanted to say, *No!* I wanted to run away and forget about everything that happened between us! But some small voice inside me permitted me to say, "Yes."

"I'll pick you up in my car around 5:30," he said. "Would you like to go to dinner somewhere? I don't want to eat at the orphanage. I want to talk with you alone. Somewhere private."

"Okay."

We couldn't think of a place to eat, so we picked up some subs and headed to a nearby park that had a lot of secluded places where we could be alone and talk.

I had the rest of the afternoon to think. My thoughts wouldn't leave me alone. What did Mike want to talk to me about? Did he want to tell me he never wants to see me again? Or did he want to tell me he was leaving the seminary to be with me? My mind was swirling, my head hurt, and I felt sick to my stomach. I wanted to take a nap to try to calm my nerves, but sleep wouldn't come. I wanted to run. I was afraid of what he was going to tell me. I was afraid either way; I didn't know what I wanted to hear. How could one kiss change the direction of my life? Did I want the direction I had chosen to change? I felt called to be a nun. I was happy with my decision and was looking forward to getting my acceptance letter. I prayed that my thoughts would stop. I needed to rest. I needed to stop trying to figure things out.

Mike picked me up on time. When I got in the car, he looked at me so tenderly.

"Are you all right?" he asked.

It took me a minute to gather my thoughts. "I'm not sure," I said.

I must have looked pretty unhappy. He reached over to hold my hand. I pulled it away. I didn't know why I did that, because I actually wanted to hold his hand. Then I realized that I was angry with him. He changed my life with just one kiss. He stirred up emotions that I didn't even know I had. I wasn't sure anymore of my feelings or my life.

While Mike drove to the park, we didn't talk much. He parked in a private place near the water and a picnic table under a shady tree. I started to feel better once we ate our chips and subs and drank our pop.

Mike started out with small talk and shared that before he left the boys, they were trying to talk Sister Mary Paul into getting a puppy. One of the other staff brought in a litter of puppies; the boys were begging and pleading for her to let them have one. Mike said Sister Mary Paul was softening, but he wasn't sure by the time he left if the boys won her over.

After we finished eating, Mike suggested that we sit by the water. He had brought a blanket with him and gestured for me to sit next to him. I felt cautious, but sat beside him anyway. He took both my hands in his and looked straight into my eyes.

"I'm sorry," he said.

I told him I was upset. Our free and easy friendship was gone.

"Everything is going to be okay," he said softly, over and over, while holding my hands and gazing at me tenderly.

"I'm as confused as I think you are," he said, "but I'm not ready to let you go. I've never had feelings like I've experienced with you ever before. I want time to search my heart and soul. And I want time with you."

"What about you becoming a priest and me a nun?" I asked.

He thought for a moment, then said in a whispery voice: "I'm not sure anymore. But I'm also not ready to say that I don't want to be a priest, either. All I know is that I don't want to stop seeing you. Do you want to see me to find out if we are meant to be together?"

"I'm not sure," I said. "How can we see each other without everyone knowing?"

"We'll find a way." He pulled me into his arms and kissed me. My body was full of emotions that overwhelmed and excited me. I started to cry. The thoughts and feelings that I'd been keeping inside me all day spilled out. Mike held me even closer.

"We have time to figure things out," he said in a reassuring tone. "We'll figure them out together."

Chapter 5

MIKE AND I SPENT the summer together whenever we could, taking walks around our favorite park, talking and talking, trying to figure out what we had together. We made out whenever we could find a place where we thought no one could see us. He was still living at the seminary, taking classes, and I was still working full time at the orphanage and taking classes at the community college.

My dear friend Jill, who lived with me on campus, took me aside one day.

"I want to talk with you," she said.

We went to my room; she shut the door so no one would disturb us.

"Is everything okay?" she asked. "You aren't your happy-go-lucky self. I can tell something is bothering you. Can I help you?"

I appreciated that my friend was concerned about me.

"Did you get your acceptance letter to the convent?" she asked. "Are you upset that maybe you weren't accepted?"

"I'm fine," I said. "I haven't received a letter yet."

"Is it Mike?" she asked.

I was taken aback! I didn't think anyone knew about us. I could feel my face getting red.

"It is Mike, isn't it?" she asked.

I told Jill everything that had happened since the magical night at summer camp and that I'd been seeing Mike whenever possible. I spilled my guts to her, from the excitement to the shame and guilt.

"I don't know what I'm going to do," I said. "Mike isn't sure if he still wants to be a priest, and I don't know if I still want to be a nun."

Jill listened with compassion and empathy; it was such a relief to share my thoughts and feelings with someone besides Mike.

"Your secret is safe with me," Jill promised. "And if you ever need to talk, I'll be there for you."

"Thank you," I said. "I will."

Mike and I met after work.

"I'm going to be gone for a week because I have to go on retreat," he said. "I don't want to go, but it's mandatory. I thought about it, and decided it would probably be best for me to go, to get some perspective on what I'm feeling."

"I think it's a good idea as well," I said.

I was so scared! I'd become so accustomed to him telling me his thoughts and feelings every time we met. But with him away, I would have no idea what he was thinking. It was unnerving; my heart was unsettled. How would I handle not being able to see him, talk to him, or know what was in his heart for a whole week?

I felt lost and alone. I wanted answers, but found none. I had to wait. I realized I hadn't taken time to be alone myself, to look into the silence of my own heart and soul to ask the hard question: "What do I want?"

I had no answers, so I went to the one place where I usually found solace and comfort: in the deep recesses of my mind, where my soul and spirit lay open to hearing the will of God. It's the place I often did ask the hard questions, the ones I was afraid to ask, but needed to. It was the place where I asked God, "Am I meant to be a nun?"

My heart seemed so shattered and torn, I didn't know anymore. I felt so unsure, so alone. I needed and wanted to be in the one place where I often found peace; I needed peace alive in my heart and soul again.

I found it in the woods, where nature was in full bloom, with wildflowers and trees dancing with the music of the wind, birds singing, squirrels running and chasing each other, frogs and fish living in harmony in a small creek. I would sometimes remove my shoes and socks to cool my feet, to feel the living water. I loved it there. It's where I found peace, where I prayed, where I sought answers and listened as Spirit whispered ever so gently and guided me.

I had gone there several times before, but not of late. Why did I stop? I didn't know. Was it because I didn't want to know God's will? I prayed and prayed that afternoon with such a sincere heart asking for the will of God to be known to me. I asked God to give me a sign and answer, "What do you want me to do?"

The next time I saw Mike was at a get-together that the nuns had for all the seminarians who worked at the orphanage along with us girls who lived on campus. Mike was wearing his priestly black suit with the clerical collar. I looked at him in shock; I had never seen him looking or dressed like a priest before. I felt overwhelmed, like I was going to pass out. I left the room, shaking. I couldn't believe he showed up looking like an ordained priest. Had he made his decision without telling me?

Jill had followed me and stopped me.

"Are you okay?" she asked.

Mike was right behind her.

"I'm sorry," he said. "I hadn't thought about how seeing me dressed as a priest would affect you. The nuns wanted to see the guys wearing their priestly suits. Can we talk later? Please come back in. Everyone is looking for you."

I got myself together and stuffed my feelings inside, where you put such things, hoping never to bring them up again. I rubbed my face, hoping to rub off what I was feeling. I put on a smiling face and went back inside.

"Are you all right?" one of the nuns asked.

"Yes," I said. "I just needed to get some cool air because it was so hot in the room."

Mike and I didn't interact much. However, he did take me aside and ask again if we could get together later that night.

"Are you sure you want to, after the way I acted?" I asked.

"That's exactly why I want to get together," he said.

A short time later, Mike drove us to our favorite place. It was dark, and it started to rain, so we stayed in the car.

Mike didn't say a word. He just looked at me, pulled me into his arms, and kissed me. I didn't know what to do. I wasn't responding. I wasn't expecting that. He must have read my mind, so he let go of me.

"I missed you so much," he said.

With that, I realized how much I missed him. We kissed as if there was no tomorrow; we weren't thinking. We were just responding to how we felt. The passion between us was strong. We were ignoring boundaries. I wasn't thinking anymore. I was feeling. Mike had his hands all over me, touching me in areas never explored before. It felt wonderful. He was touching my breasts, kissing my neck, my ears. He pushed my bra away from my breast so he could touch my naked skin.

He kissed and caressed my breast, leaving me disoriented, lost in the moment. Mike took my hand and put it down his pants, where I felt his erect penis. I pulled my hand away so fast, as if I had touched a hot stove. I started crying.

"Stop," I said.

He did, and held me.

"I'm so sorry," Mike said. "I don't seem to have control of myself when it comes to you."

"We're going too far," I said. "It unnerves me."

"I agree," Mike said. "I promise to never go that far again."

We did kiss a little more and held each other close, while thoughts swirled in my head. I was so confused by my passion and desires, and with the unresolved issue of my life, our life. I was afraid; something inside my stomach hurt.

The next morning I awoke only to discover my body covered in hives from head to foot. I mean big, red, swollen hives. I went to Jill's room.

"What happened?"

"I don't know."

"Is this from seeing Mike dressed as a priest?" she asked. "Was it something you ate? Did you hear if you were accepted into the convent?"

"It could be all of that," I said.

I went to work. When Sister Mary Paul saw me, she sent me to the clinic to get checked out.

"It could be a reaction to something you ate," the doctor said, "or it could be stress-related. Are you under any stress?"

"I don't think so," I lied.

He gave me some medication; it took almost a full week for the hives to go away. It seemed like every time I was with Mike and getting passionate, I would start to break out in hives again. Talk about a sign!

Mike and I continued to see each other, but curtailed our passion. The summer was coming to an end. I still hadn't heard if I was accepted into the convent. Mike would be leaving to return full time to the seminary, still not knowing what to do about us or the priesthood. I so cared for him, but I felt so guilty about our relationship. I felt like we crossed the line so many times. Shame filled my uncertain heart. What did God want of me? That question lay in the back of my mind like a dream that needed to awaken. It didn't seem fair to either one of us.

I couldn't help but think we should have ended it before it got this far.

Chapter 6

It was the end of my morning shift at the orphanage when Sister Mary Paul asked that I meet with her in the orphanage's chapel. I felt a pain in the pit of my stomach. Why did she want to see me in the chapel? Did she find out about my relationship with Mike? I tried to shove my thoughts and fears to the back of my mind.

When my shift was over, I walked slowly down the hall toward the chapel, my head bent down in thought, each step bringing me closer to the unknown. My heart was beating so fast, I was unconsciously rubbing my increasingly sweaty palms together.

When I opened the doors, I found a chapel full of nuns all looking at me. I must have looked frightened, because Sister Mary Ann took my hand and said, "We have something for you." She handed me an envelope from the Mother House; it was unopened.

"Hurry up," one of the nuns said. "We're all anxious to find out what it says."

Sister Margaret Ann, the Mother Superior, already knew, but didn't say anything to the other sisters.

"Calm down," she told them. "It's for Lin."

I looked at the envelope, thinking, *Here it goes...* I didn't think this day was ever going to come. As I pulled the letter out of the envelope, one of the other nuns suggested, "Read it out loud." Mother

Superior in her Mother Superior voice, again said, "Let her read it first. Then if she wants, she can share it with all of you."

I silently read the first several lines; nothing yet stated if I was accepted or not. Then, there it was.

I was accepted to the order of the Sisters of Divine Love. The tears came like a waterfall running down my face; I had waited for so long. I fell to my knees and said, "Thank you, God."

And with that, all the Sisters joined in a chorus of celebration, giving hugs and congratulating me. It was so overwhelming and wonderful. My heart was beating so fast and joyfully, as if on a joy ride. I didn't know how to react; I felt frozen in time. As the smile on my face grew ever so wide, I kept repeating to myself silently as a gentle whisper in my mind: "I was accepted!"

Just then, one of the sisters took the letter from my hand and read it out loud so everyone could hear. I was so happy! It was like all the doubt, confusion, and fear all summer had disappeared like a vanishing wind storm. I was ecstatic. I wanted to shout from the highest mountain: "I was accepted into the order of the Sisters of Divine Love."

Sister Mary Ann walked with me to a lunch celebration that Sister Margaret Ann had planned for me. She invited all the nuns and some of the girls I lived with on campus to join us. Jill came running up and congratulated me with a hug.

"I'm so happy for you!" Jill was the only one who knew how much I wanted to find out whether I was accepted into the convent.

Lunch was fabulous, and afterward, my stomach was as full as my thankful heart. Jill walked with me back to our place on campus. We made small talk, and then…she asked about Mike.

Mike!

"I haven't even thought of him all day," I confessed. It seemed unusual because Mike was always on my mind. The memories of the time on the dock returned like an unwanted friend from the place where shame, confusion, fear, and passion lived. I wanted to forget about all that.

"Does Mike know?" Jill asked.

"No, I just found out this morning, and I thought maybe Sister Margaret Ann told him." That thought quickly left my mind because she didn't tell any of the nuns before I knew.

"What are you going to do?" Jill asked. "You seemed so happy with the news of being accepted into the convent."

"I can't remember being so happy. I feel so blessed, so at peace. I was called by God." I found it difficult to explain to her what I was feeling — such a deep warmth of unconditional love and excitement, as if all the angels were celebrating with me. I found myself in love.

The weekend was coming up in a few days, and I knew I had to tell Mike of my acceptance letter. I went to my favorite place in the woods to think of how I was going to tell him, to search my soul, my heart. I found myself crying and crying as the once joyous feeling of going into the convent was met with, "Oh my God, what am I going to do?" I was so bewildered, unable to think clearly. I couldn't pray or even ask God for help. I was left alone to cry, to try and figure out how and what I was going to tell Mike. I left my once-peaceful wooded area with no answers. My head was throbbing. My heart ached. My God left me alone. I needed to do this one myself, but I didn't know how.

Back in my room, Jill knocked on the door. I almost didn't answer, but I thought she saw me coming into the building, so I told her to come in. Jill just took one look at me and asked, "What happened?"

She, too, was confused; I had been so happy, and now I looked like someone died. Like always, I felt at ease with Jill and told her I didn't know how I was going to tell Mike.

"I'm glad I'm not in your shoes," Jill said.

"I wish I weren't in my shoes."

"Do you want to continue with the pain and turmoil, or would it be better to call Mike and ask to see him sooner?" she asked.

"I don't know if I can ever tell him."

"Do you truly want to go to the convent or not?" Jill asked. "I've never seen you as happy as you were at lunch. You were beaming with happiness and joy. Did you ever feel that way when you were with Mike?"

A part of me wished she hadn't asked me that. I didn't want to know the answer. My body was filled with anguish and pain. I cried until I couldn't cry anymore. Jill held me like a child. I was scared, so unhappy. I didn't want to feel this.

"Take some time," Jill suggested, "but not too long, to figure out what you want."

I pulled away, like out of a trance, saying, "I know what I want. I just don't know how to tell Mike."

The next morning, I woke up knowing I had to call Mike.

"Do you have some time to see me after work?"

"You've heard," Mike said.

"I did. I want to see you if you're free."

"I can come, but not until after my eight o'clock class," he said with a concerned tone. "Do you want to go to the park?"

I hesitated, then said no.

"I want to take you to my favorite place on campus," I said. "It's a place I've never taken or shared with you before, but I want to now."

Mike was quiet. "I'm going to skip my evening class. Can you get off work earlier? I'm concerned about it getting dark."

"I'll ask Jill," I said, because I knew she wasn't working the afternoon shift.

Jill agreed. When Mike and I met at the front of the orphanage, he had a weak smile and a worried look on his face. I think I looked about the same. He went to hold my hand, but I pulled it away; not so much as I didn't want to hold his hand, but because I didn't want any of the nuns to see us holding hands.

I took him to my little paradise on campus.

"I'm amazed at its simple beauty and peacefulness," he said. "I understand why you love it here so much."

We sat where I always sat alone with my thoughts and dreams, only now I was sharing it with him. I found myself wanting to cry, but tears wouldn't come. I was so sad. Mike held me tenderly as if knowing he would never hold me like that again. He kissed me. I let him kiss me, but something in me was gone. It was then that I truly knew what I needed to do and to tell him about my decision.

"I love you so much, Mike," I said. " I need to find out if I am meant to be a nun. I need to find out if God is calling me to religious life. If I don't give religious life a chance, I will always question whether I was meant to be a nun or not."

Mike's eyes filled with tears, as we held each other and cried. I was not only crying over my love for Mike, but also for the relief I felt by telling him my decision.

"I respect you and I love you," Mike said. "I want you to be happy. And part of me understands."

Then he told me that he had made his decision to leave the

priesthood. "I didn't want to tell you until you heard and made your own decision about religious life."

I will never forget that night or any of the days and evenings we were together. Nor will I forget his welcoming care and tenderness or his unselfish love. A part of me will always love Mike; he was truly my first love.

I was sad for several days after our time in the woods. I wanted to be alone; I felt wounded. The sadness was like a blackened cloud; it finally left me, replaced with the business of getting ready to leave for the convent.

Chapter 7

I FINALLY TOLD MY parents and family about my decision, and they seemed happy for me. I think my dad said something jokingly like, "It's about time you make something of yourself!"

I took it in good humor, but later thought about it. I was going to be leaving in a few weeks and had a million and one things to do. The sisters had given me a list of things I needed to bring, such as a black traveling trunk — like the kind that passengers took on the Titanic — to keep all my things.

Everything I would ever own would need to fit in that black trunk for all the days of my life. I needed to buy nunny underwear, bras, black shoes, black tights, a black robe, a black coat. Black, black, black. I was never going to wear anything colorful again.

My mother and father thought they were going to drive me to St. Louis on September 18th, as stated in the letter provided to all the parents. The letter said it was the parents' responsibility to get their daughter to the Mother House. I was surprised when Sister Mary Ann said she just got off the phone with my parents, and that they would be coming by to drop off my things. Sister Mary Ann explained that a few of the sisters, including herself, were going to be going to the Mother House and suggested I ride with them. I was surprised and pleased because driving with my parents all the way to St. Louis was not something I wanted to do.

"I thought you'd be happy," Sister Mary Ann said with a wink and a smile. She knew a little of my home life, but not much. I didn't like talking about my parents and kept most things to myself. I guess Sister Mary Ann knew enough to make sure my entrance into the convent would be as peaceful as possible.

My parents dropped off my things, then we went out to dinner. It was unsettling; I had so many unresolved issues with them, and yet I felt sad. My mother's mental illness didn't help; I remember when I was a child how I was able to calm the ugly beast that lived inside her by telling her, "You're so wonderful. I love you more than anything else." Those simple words calmed her, but not always. I never knew what beast would be hiding behind those eyes of hers. My father was emotionally absent, and I always got the impression that he didn't like me. For some reason, I was afraid of him. He never beat us as my mother did, but I was still afraid to be alone with him.

I was going to be leaving them to start my own new life in the convent. I was happy about going, but I had mixed feelings. I wouldn't see them for a year until I completed my postulancy, which is "A person taking the first step in religious life before entering the novitiate and receiving the habit," according to catholicculture.org. "The purpose of the postulancy is to acquire some knowledge of the religious life and of the particular institute through personal experience. It enables one to become better known to the superiors of the community, and to develop such virtue as will qualify the candidate for acceptance into the novitiate." [1]

---

[1] https://www.catholicculture.org/culture/library/dictionary/index.cfm?id=35671

If anything happened to my parents during that time, I wouldn't be able to come home. When we returned to the orphanage, it was time to say goodbye.

I hugged them with tears and a lump in my throat.

"I love you. I'm going to miss you."

"We're proud of you," my parents said. "We hope you'll be happy."

After this bittersweet farewell, Sister Mary Ann asked some of the other sisters to help get my things in the car. We would be leaving very early the next morning.

"How are you?" Sister Mary Ann asked. "It's always difficult saying goodbye."

I just shook my head. I didn't want her to see how upset I really was. I was leaving everything I knew behind to start a new life, a life I knew very little about. But I was comforted knowing the sisters would be with me on my journey.

I slept in the sisters' quarters at the orphanage that night, alone with only my thoughts to keep me company. I prayed and prayed. I even said the rosary, hoping to fall asleep, but sleep would not come to me. I was too anxious. Everything was so new, so strange, so unknown.

Chapter 8

THE SISTERS WOKE ME up by singing; they stood outside my door and sang a beautiful song I hadn't heard before. I went to the door looking like God knows what and said, "Good morning."

It was still dark outside. I don't think I got any sleep. The sisters said they would meet me in the chapel for Mass in about an hour. I dressed and met them as instructed.

After Mass, Sister Mary Paul had all the boys that I worked with that summer meet me in chapel to say goodbye. It was so much harder saying goodbye to my beloved boys than it was to my family. I realized that these children had become a part of my family in such a short time. Each boy kissed me and gave me a card personally made just for me; they said I could read the cards when I got to St. Louis, at the prompting of Sister Mary Paul. I cried with each boy as I kissed them goodbye, telling them how much I would miss them, and how much I loved them. One of my favorite boys brought Vincent, the dog, to say goodbye. That was it; I was crying so hard I couldn't catch my breath. That's when Sister Mary Paul wrapped her arms around me and simply said, "Thank you. I don't know what I would have done without your help this summer. You were such a joy to work with."

And with that, I was whisked off to the car. Sister Mary Ann said we would stop and eat on the way to St. Louis. "You need some time to settle down," she said. "And besides, the nuns rarely eat out. They're looking forward to it."

The drive to St. Louis was long and uneventful. I fell asleep in the back seat with my mouth wide open with drool running down the side of my mouth. When I woke up, embarrassed, I wiped the sides of my mouth. Sister Mary Ann saw me from the rearview mirror and smiled.

She gestured for me to take a look at the two sleeping nuns next to me in the back seat, as if to say I had nothing to be embarrassed about.

We finally arrived at the Mother House; it was then that I realized my decision to enter the convent was real. I felt a tightening in my chest. My mouth was dry, and I was finding it difficult to swallow. The Mother House looked like a castle in New England, with large, dark, wooden doors that were too heavy for one person to open by themselves. Large stained glass windows depicted the lives of the Saints, Christ, Mary, and the order of the Sisters of Divine Love. I was in awe of this magnificent building. It was difficult for me to wrap my mind around the fact that this was going to be my home for the next several years.

I was so busy looking through the window in awe, I remained in the car after the other sisters had gotten out. Sister Mary Ann opened the car door and said, "It's time."

I couldn't feel my feet on the ground. I felt numb. My legs were weak as I followed the sisters up the numerous steps leading to the entrance of my new life. I wasn't sure I would be able to reach the top of the stairs without fainting.

Once in the building, several other sisters came to greet us, all smiling as if old friends had just returned home. I realized that Sister

Mary Ann and the other sisters *were* returning home, for they too lived at the Mother House during their formation years. One of the sisters suggested the other sisters get settled in their rooms. We were instructed to meet in the chapel at 5:00 p.m. I stood there alone, lost, not knowing what I was supposed to do, when a young, smiling sister approached me and suggested I follow her.

She took me to a simple room where I was to change out of my lay clothes and put on the clothes laid out on the bed. I didn't realize it at the time, but that tiny, simple room was going to be my bedroom. Another sister entered and introduced herself as my new Superior, Sister Elizabeth Marie; she would be responsible for the formation of my postulancy for the next year. Sister Elizabeth Marie was pretty; she was young with a great smile and a warm personality. I liked her right away.

"Hurry up and change," she said. "Another sister will come and get you in about 20 minutes."

I changed my clothes and put on the habit I would be wearing for the next year. I went to look at myself, but found no mirror. I sat on the side of the bed in silence, and just looked at those sterile white walls with a wooden crucifix staring at me. My traveling black trunk and guitar were in the corner. I felt numb with a slight nervous headache.

The sister whom Sister Elizabeth Marie said would get me in 20 minutes was right on time. She, too, was young and cheerful. She told me her name, but I couldn't remember it; everything was a blur.

"You'll be meeting the other girls who will be your formation group," she said.

I was escorted to the chapel wearing the habit of a young postulant. I knew my feet were moving, but I couldn't feel the floor. I felt like I was floating, having an out-of-body experience.

Once in the chapel, each of us eight girls was lined up in a single file holding a candle and a wooden box with a cross engraved in the center. We were led slowly down the aisle by Sister Elizabeth Marie, the Mother Superior of Postulants, to the altar. Father Matthew blessed each of us with the sign of the cross and blessed our boxes. After the blessing, Sister Elizabeth Marie placed a veil on our heads and gave us our religious names. I was named Sister Lin Marie. Once all of us girls were blessed, given our veils and names, the sisters commenced in song. The sound of the sisters' voices still brings tears to my eyes. The memory rouses a profound feeling of oneness.

After the ceremonies, I was finally introduced to my fellow Postulants. We were all around the same age — 18 to 20. Sister Mary Beth was the oldest. She had already finished college and was teaching. I liked her right away, along with several others. Some of the others seemed too nunny for me. We went on a tour of the convent and received our daily schedule, including what time to get up in the morning: five o'clock. Morning prayers were at 6:00 a.m., Mass at 7:00 a.m., breakfast at 8:00 a.m., followed by morning chores, then college classes at 9:00 a.m. We were given a map, just in case we got lost. It didn't help me much, because I couldn't read a map.

The first several months of my postulancy were all about training: learning prayers, how to sit, stand, kneel, eat, walk, talk, et cetera, and everything I needed to know about how to act like a nun. I realized that was why they called it our formation years. Sometimes I felt like I was in the military.

However, I loved my new life and everything about it. I felt such a communion with the sisters. The only thing I didn't like about it was getting up so early. Allow me to tell you a story: I was about six months into my postulancy when I was asked to ring the bell to wake the sisters up in the morning. Each sister would rotate turns, and this would be my first. The way it was supposed to go was: a sister would ring the bell at each door of the sister's bedroom and say, "Jesus lives." She would then wait to hear the sister reply, "Forever in my heart." Once the sister replied, she would go to the next bedroom.

Now it is important to remember how much I hated getting up so early, and I had to get up earlier to wake the rest of the sisters. I was so nervous; the halls were dark except for a small light coming from a Blessed Mother statue. I started to ring the bell and forgot what I was supposed to say; the only thing I could think of was that it was morning, and I needed to wake these sisters up. So instead of saying, "Jesus lives," I went down the hall saying, "Jesus is awake, Jesus is awake." Needless to say, my Superiors were not happy with me, but some of my fellow sisters couldn't help but tease me and give me a hard time about it.

"What are we supposed to say when it's my turn to wake the sisters?" they asked playfully. They thought it was hilarious.

That year as a Postulant went by fast and I learned as much as I could about being a well-trained nun. I still struggled with being on time for prayers, learning where I was supposed to be, and talking when I wasn't supposed to. Just like grade school and high school, I was liked by my fellow sisters and was blessed with a good sense of humor. I remember dressing up as a pregnant nun for Halloween. I won't tell you what happened to me after that incident. I think I got away with a lot of things because I was the only one who played the guitar and was teaching some of the other sisters, including Sister Elizabeth Marie, my Superior. I had written several songs we sang at Mass and would be sent to other convents in the area to teach them, especially if a holiday or feast day were coming up, when all the nuns would be coming back to the Mother House. I remember the first time I heard one of the songs I wrote being sung by more than one hundred nuns. It was humbling, but I knew that the songs came from a place inside me where Spirit lived, as I always felt divinely inspired.

After my year as a postulant, I became a novice sister and wore the full habit with a white veil. Being in the novitiate meant a year of silence and prayer. It was a period of preparation for taking vows and to discern whether one was called to religious life. This year was the hardest for me because I loved to talk and whenever some of us got the chance, we would sneak off and talk about anything, just to talk to someone. Our college classes were restricted to religious ones, such as New and Old Testament, church history, and theology classes. I was majoring in psychology with a required minor in theology.

My year as a novice sister went by slowly, and I learned that being prohibited to talk messed with my mind. I sang a lot that year, wrote a lot more songs, and came up with every excuse that we sisters needed to practice.

Let me go back a minute; I think some of you might be wondering what was in those wooden boxes given to us our first night. The boxes contained two rosaries — one long one that hung on the side of the habit, and one smaller one we kept in our pocket. They also contained prayer books — one for morning prayers and one for evening prayers — and a journal. I'm not going to go into much more about my convent days because this book isn't really about that. I will share, however, why I was asked to leave the convent and how that affected my life.

Chapter 9

I WAS AT THE wrong place at the wrong time, as the saying goes. I was asked to get something from the pantry when I walked into a scene that shocked me. I saw two of my superiors kissing! They were kissing each other like Mike and I once kissed. They saw me, and I definitely saw them. I ran out of the room to find the closest door leading to the outside. I needed to breathe. I ran all the way to the cemetery crying. I couldn't believe what I saw. It scared me to my core. I was shaking so hard, I thought I was going to pass out. I sat down next to an old, large oak tree where I held my head in my hands. My knees bent to my chest in a fetal position. I couldn't move. Fear swelled up in me as if I were beaten; I felt trapped, unable to move.

Then I heard a voice. It was one of the sisters I saw kissing; she called my name and told me to follow her. I couldn't move. I couldn't talk. I was numb with fear.

"Look at me!" she said with a frustrated tone.

I still couldn't move.

"I want to see you in chapel in one hour," she said. I didn't go to meet her, but later that evening I did leave a note on her desk that announced, "I am placing myself on Grand Silence." If a sister puts herself on Grand Silence, it was because she was thinking of leaving the convent or because she needed to make some other important decision. She would not talk to anyone, nor could anyone talk to her, until she took herself off of Grand Silence. I wasn't talking to anyone. I wasn't able to sleep. I wasn't able to shake my feelings of fear. Somehow I felt it was my fault; I felt ashamed. Fear overwhelmed me. I didn't understand what frightened me; I just was afraid.

Three days after I saw the sisters kissing, they found me in the chapel and approached me.

"We, too, have been praying, and the Holy Spirit told us that you would make a better wife and mother, and that you would be leaving in the morning," they said.

I couldn't make eye contact. I kept my head down. When I finally found my voice, I told them I wanted to meet with the Mother Superior. The sisters told me they had already spoken to her and she agreed it was better that I leave. I didn't cry. I wasn't even upset. I was in shock. I couldn't understand why I had to leave; I didn't do anything except see something I shouldn't have seen. But one of the main rules that all good nuns knew was not to question. It's called the vow of obedience. I did as I was told and left early that next morning.

I left the convent wearing my habit; I wasn't permitted to say goodbye to any of my fellow sisters. My trunk with all my possessions and my guitar were waiting in the hall.

"You'll be taking a train back to the orphanage," one of the sisters told me. "Someone will pick you up."

As I was leaving, one of the older sisters came up to me, hugged me, and whispered in my ear, "You will always be a sister of Divine Love."

And with that, I was taken to the train station and placed on the train. The ride back was long and draining; I didn't know what I was feeling. I worked hard not to show any emotions on the train since people were looking at me. People always stared at nuns. I acted like

I was sleeping and kept my eyes closed most of the time. I was numb, devastated, lost in grief. I must have fallen asleep, because someone woke me to tell me they thought I was at my destination.

I was relieved when I saw my dearest friend, Sister Mary Ann. She got my things and put them in the back of the car.

"The sisters are so concerned," she said. "All they know is that you're returning with no reason or explanation given."

Then Sister Mary Ann suggested we go for a walk or find somewhere we could talk before returning to the orphanage.

"Sister Lin Marie," she said gently, "please tell me what was going on. You look like hell."

I was too embarrassed to tell. I felt so much shame, almost like I was the one who committed the act. Fear seemed to swallow me whole with no escape.

"You need to get some rest and get something to eat," Sister Mary Ann suggested. She stayed with me, waiting for me to talk if I wanted to. I didn't want to talk about the incident, nor did I think I ever would.

"You'll be staying with the sisters until you feel better," Sister Mary Ann said. It was late when she left me. "Sleep in as long as you need to in the morning. Don't worry about morning prayers or Mass."

I slept surprisingly well, waking up in time for Mass. I joined the sisters in chapel, feeling like I was home again. The sisters were kind. No one asked any questions, but I knew they wanted to know why I was back. They were confused; they had only heard how great everything was going. They'd heard about the songs I wrote, and it seemed everything was going well for their young sister. They were so proud of me. I felt like I let them down, but I couldn't tell them why I was asked to leave. I just couldn't.

I stayed working at the orphanage for a few months to make some money and get my life back on track. My good friend Jill and I hung out; she helped me buy clothes and get back to living as a layperson again.

No, I did not hear from Mike. I did hear that he was getting married. My heart sunk a little, but I let it go.

Chapter 10

I LEFT THE ORPHANAGE and got a job at another children's group home in the area. It was much smaller. At full capacity, it housed 20 children. We specialized in keeping siblings together while parents were incarcerated or if the children were removed from the home because of abuse. Back in the day, most all staff lived with the children and worked a 24-hour shift with two days off each week. I was the staff supervisor and was in charge of scheduling the day-to-day activities of the group home. This included coordinating staffing hours and days off; finding schools for the children; counseling, et cetera. The children's ages ranged from two to 14, and many had severe behavioral issues. I loved that job, and the staff I supervised were wonderful and easy to work with. Most of the staff were women, but I did have a couple of male staff as well.

The director, Helen, was my mother's age, and we got along really well. We spent many hours discussing treatment plans for the children, as well as providing training for the staff. We spent many late hours, after the children were asleep, working in her living quarters with a glass of wine or two after an exhausting day. The children's severe behavioral issues caused fear that made them act out. Helen was devoted to the children, myself, and the staff; she would do anything she could to make our jobs easier.

On one particular night, I felt more exhausted than usual and had a small headache; I told Helen that I would meet her later in her living quarters — after the children were asleep — to discuss the day's events.

When I arrived, Helen took one look at me and said, "You need some wine. How are you feeling?"

"I have a slight headache."

"Sit in this chair," she said, proceeding to give me a head and neck massage.

"That feels wonderful," I said. That, plus the wine was relaxing me.

Helen moved in front of me and started to rub my forehead and cheekbones. Within seconds, she was kissing me. I jumped out of that chair and out of her living quarters so fast — as if I just got an electric shock. It was a shock indeed!

I was shaking when I got to my living quarters. I could barely breathe. And I burst into tears.

"Please let me in," Helen asked from the other side of my shut door. I let her in because she was my boss, and I guess with the training from the convent, I obeyed.

"I'm sorry," Helen said. "I misread you. I thought you were enjoying me touching you."

"I did enjoy the massage, but please don't ever kiss me again."

Helen was embarrassed. Part of me felt bad for her.

"I want to make sure my behavior didn't change things between us. We make such a good team."

"I need some time to think," I said.

"I promise I'll never try something like that again," she said. "I thought we could still be friends."

a spiritual journey

I didn't want her upset with me. I wanted things to be as they were before.

"Thank you," Helen said and left my room.

I was still shaking, my stomach hurt, and the headache was back in full force.

It took a few days before Helen and I were back to the daily routine of caring for the children and staff. I missed how well we worked together. I began to feel more comfortable around Helen again, and it felt okay to meet with her in her living quarters, and to be honest, I missed the wine, too.

I found myself thinking of her kiss and found it shocking that I liked it. I didn't know what to do with such thoughts and feelings, so I decided I needed to get into therapy right away. I knew my feelings were wrong and I needed help. I called one of the clinics that had a good reputation, and made an appointment to meet on my next day off.

The days leading up to therapy were difficult; I was vacillating back and forth whether I needed to go to therapy or not. I couldn't imagine me telling the therapist the real reason I was there. The day finally came, so I put one foot in front of the other and took the difficult leap into therapy.

I liked my therapist Kathy right away. With kind blue eyes and a warm, friendly smile, she was very professional.

"Why are you seeking therapy," she asked. "And how do you think I can help?"

"I was in the convent and was having problems adjusting," I said.

Then I thought, *How smart was that? Lying to the therapist right off the bat?* Then I realized I did have issues about leaving the convent.

"Part of me was devastated when I was asked to leave the convent, taken from the life I felt so called to," I said. "The church says, 'Many are called, but few are chosen' to religious life." At some level, I felt God didn't want or love me either. Why wasn't I called? Was it because of Mike? Was it because of my feelings towards him? Was God punishing me? I did tell Kathy the reason that I was asked to leave and how it affected me. We had several sessions discussing my feelings on the subject, but I never felt it was resolved or worked through enough to bring me peace. Instead, my abrupt expulsion from the convent made me feel abandoned and alone.

Kathy and I worked well together. She often gave me suggestions on different treatments and techniques, which proved beneficial with the children I worked with. I met with her biweekly because I couldn't afford to meet with her weekly.

"It's time to get to the real reason for therapy," Kathy said after several months. "I think you're holding back."

I was, but I was afraid to tell her about the kiss and my liking it. I liked Kathy, and I didn't want her to dislike me.

"You can tell me anything," she said, "and I won't judge you. You're paying me to help you, so you need to open up and trust me."

It took another couple of appointments for me to open up and finally tell her about the kiss and my feelings.

She was so gracious and understanding.

"You don't need to worry about the kiss or the feelings you're experiencing," she said. Then in a gentle voice, she asked, "What are you really afraid of?"

I started to cry, then said, "I don't want to be gay."

She let me cry. "There is nothing wrong with being gay."

"I don't want to be gay," I repeated. In my eyes, at the time, I believed it was a sin, and abnormal, to be gay.

This exchange prompted Kathy to want me to see her weekly. Helen allowed me to work some extra hours on the weekends so I could afford therapy. Meanwhile, I thought I was doing better, much better, in fact. I was beginning to realize I was not gay.

At my next therapy session, Kathy dropped a bombshell: "I think you're still holding something back."

"I'm not," I said. "I've told you everything."

"I want to try hypnotherapy to help you let go of whatever it is that you're afraid to share," she said.

I agreed because I knew there couldn't be anything else. But the hypnotherapy didn't work. The next week, Kathy greeted me at the door and escorted me to another room at the clinic; the room was dark with soft tones of light and soft music playing. She offered me an alcoholic drink; I think it was whiskey.

"This might help you relax," she said.

It must have worked, because the next thing I knew I was talking. I remember telling her that my father was touching me and doing things sexually to me and wanting me to do things to him. When the hypnosis was over, I sat in silence wondering why I said what I said; I didn't believe it. I never went back to therapy, until many years later.

Chapter 11

I SPENT SEVERAL YEARS searching, always looking for love, wanting to feel love, and aching to know love. I took different paths on my quest to find what would fill my empty soul. Some paths were spiritual and temporarily fulfilling. Other roads led to days void of consciousness toward anything in particular. I drifted from one relationship to another, hoping to feel something, but I only ached with disappointment every time.

Perhaps you've walked a similar journey. I'm sharing mine now, hoping that you can glean some understanding that propels you toward the best destination for your life.

After leaving the convent, the Church, and therapy, I felt empty, so I went searching — not consciously at the time — with the hope of finding myself... and some meaning in my life.

I stopped working at the orphanage and got a job at a Detroit psychiatric hospital for a few years.

One day a friend asked, "Would you like to attend a workshop on higher consciousness to learn how to awaken yourself to serenity and self-discovery?"

Why not? I thought.

Working the afternoon shift at the psychiatric hospital was becoming more difficult, because I was getting beaten up by some patients. They didn't mean to do what they did. Sadly, they were lost souls imprisoned in a life haunted by voices and demons that never relented until the medication started working and then they could hope again to be normal (whatever that is). I felt blessed to be working with people who had a diagnosis of mental illness. I felt I had a deeper understanding of how difficult life was for them. Their minds and heads filled with never-ending voices, not their own. Always telling them what they should or should not do, never trusting anyone.

I have a profound and deep appreciation for people who suffered from mental illness, whose daily struggle was sometimes just being able to get up in the morning, knowing that's the best they can do. I so remember those days with my mother; unfortunately, I didn't have the understanding I do now.

I was ready to try another adventure to find some truth that would awaken my spirit. My soul was always looking for some inner peace, some deeper meaning for my existence. When I attended the workshop with my friend, I liked what I heard as it registered somewhere in my awareness that this is something I wanted to learn more and become a part of.

The instructor, called Sharer, stated that if anyone was interested in learning more about the life and the teachings of Ken Keyes and if one felt called to experience life at a deeper more conscious level, then they are welcome to come and live at Cornucopia.

I left Michigan to attend a place called Cornucopia in Kentucky, where I took the name of Surrender. I was learning the teachings of Ken Keyes, who wrote the book *Handbook for Higher Consciousness*. I lived in a community with like-minded people, a commune if you like, of adults and children.

It wasn't that different from being back in the convent: we all got up early each morning, but instead of prayers in a chapel, we meditated outside by taking morning walks. Each morning, rain or shine, we welcomed a beautiful panoramic view of rolling hills, thick green forests, flowing rivers, serene lakes, and majestic mountains. Mother Nature was alive and well. Seeing beautiful grounds every day that would at times take my breath away, I never tired of its beauty nor took its splendor for granted.

I meditated to the beauty and sounds of nature. Often while listening to the birds sing their welcoming morning songs, I found myself wanting to and did at times sing along with them.

We all had daily chores. I worked with the children and took classes to become a Sharer, or an instructor at the workshops. Most of the others who lived at Cornucopia didn't want to be a Sharer, they simply wanted to live the simple communal lifestyle and follow the teachings of Ken Keyes.

The first year at Cornucopia was all about training. No sexual relationships were allowed. The teaching was that one needed to work on themselves first, not a relationship. After my first year of training, I became close to several people while living at Cornucopia and had a couple of very brief sexual encounters with both men and women. Women, I know, so shocking. Something always seemed to hold me back; I never really felt safe. I still loved kissing and going to first base so to speak but anything more than that caused anxiety.

I continuously told myself: *I'm here to work on myself, not a relationship.* However, somewhere in my lost heart, I so wanted to allow love in. I stayed and lived at Cornucopia for another year until they closed. The lease on the property expired, and everyone had to leave.

Many of us moved to California to follow yet another teaching of Bhagwan Rajneesh — a mystic, a guru, and spiritual teacher. My name was Antra Mangala. They told me that it meant: "one who is on the move." I wore light cotton, orange clothes resembling a Buddhist monk's robe with Birkenstock sandals. Again, much like my convent days, we all wore the same clothes, and instead of a cross around our necks, was a necklace of beads with a picture of Rajneesh.

I stayed at the ashram for a very short time; I didn't like many of the practices, especially the orgies, which were supposed to free us of ourselves. I did participate in one due to peer pressure. I felt like I was in the pits of hell, as bodies intertwined with each other, seeming as if in some trance or high on pot. The sounds coming from those around me was horrifying. At one point, I was laying on the floor sobbing and terrified, thinking I was going to be swallowed up by some demon, trying to find a way out, trying to get bare bodies off of me. I felt like I was going to die. The smell was putrid and sickening. I was living a nightmare, only it was real. One of my friends saw me and carried me out. I wanted to die. The fear was overwhelming, as if drowning in a sea of madness.

I left that night with some of my friends from Cornucopia. We were now homeless with only the money in our pockets. We wanted out of the confines of the ashram and the teachings of Rajneesh. He talked about love, but did not practice what he taught. It was very confusing because his teachings seemed false and didn't seem to be coming from anything but making money.

I was terrified and scared. I had never experienced anything so outrageous and disturbing. It took me a while to come to terms with my feelings. I lacked confidence. I distrusted my intuition. Prior to

a spirtual journey

this, I had always felt assured and believed that nothing this close to falling into darkness would ever happen to me on my search. I always prayed that I would never experience things that would be dangerous or harmful to my soul, yet this one came close. It took a while to forgive myself, but with the help of my Spirit guides and the love of God, I began my search again to find some meaning and purpose in my life.

Chapter 12

I WAS SO GRATEFUL to God that my work experience and degree made it easy to find a job. I lived in California for two years, loving the ocean and the mountains, the carefree life that can only happen in California. Life was good until I got news that my mother was very ill. My family thought she was going to die, and I needed to return home.

So I said goodbye to the ocean, the mountains, and good friends. My stay in California had not included any sexual relationships, and the experience with Rajneesh left me in the dead zone. I was fearful, yet had trouble identifying the source of angst that consumed me.

I went back to Michigan, to the home of my birth, to the bedroom I shared with my sister until she married and left home when I was in junior high school. It was so strange being back home. It felt cold and empty, void of life. I just stood there wanting to feel something besides sadness and loss.

"Your mother is in the hospital on a ventilator," my neighbor said.

I didn't know what to feel. My mother had always been so sick, so depressed, so unhappy most of her life. My heart broke for her. Was she finally giving up on life?

She was still young, only in her early fifties. I wanted her to be well. I wanted her to be like she was on her good days — able to be happy and smile.

At the hospital, I went to her bedside and held her hand.

"I love you," I said. "I missed you."

Tears filled her eyes. The ventilator made her unable to speak, so she wrote on a pad of paper that she was happy to see me, and that she had been waiting for me to come. I held her skeleton-like body as tears filled my eyes. She was so frail, so vulnerable, so weak, so drained of life.

"Where's Dad?"

She shook her head, indicating she didn't know.

I found my dad at the nurse's station, trying to get information. When he saw me, he looked angry and said: "It's about time."

I didn't want to hug him, so I didn't.

I hurried back to my mother. We were silent. I wanted information about her condition, but I didn't want to hear it from my dad. This amplified the strange relationships between myself and each of my parents. I never felt like I was home when I came home for visits.

"Where are you going to stay?" my father finally asked.

"I haven't thought about it," I said.

"You'll stay with me," he said. "I need your help around the house with your mother being in the hospital."

I didn't respond. He must have read my mind because he said, "I told you. You'll be staying at home. It's about time you start thinking about your parents instead of running off doing whatever you do."

He didn't know or care about what I was doing. It was always all about him.

I lived at home for almost six months and got my job back at the psychiatric hospital in Detroit. My routine was to visit my mother every afternoon after work for a couple of hours; come home and make dinner for my father; clean house; do laundry; and return to the hospital until visiting hours ended. While doing this for six months, I kept my distance from my father. I never trusted him for some reason still unknown to me. I never revisited the abuse that came out during my hypnotherapy so many years earlier, mainly because I didn't believe it.

Living at home with him was taking an emotional toll on me; he was making sexual comments that made me very uncomfortable. On the surface, I let it go.

The reality was that such behavior and thoughts were sinking into a deep, dark place inside me, where they stayed hidden, unacknowledged, and unfelt.

Chapter 13

ONE WEEKEND, AFTER VISITING my mother, I met up with some friends who introduced me to the teachings of *A Course in Miracles* by Helen Schucman.

I was fascinated by this course based on the 1976 book that aims to help individuals achieve spiritual transformation. The course teaches that the real world, which reflects truth, can be seen only through spiritual vision, and not through the body's eyes. The world of knowledge is one of unity, love, sinlessness, and abundance. *A Course* views reality as composed only of God's thoughts, which are loving, constant, timeless, and eternal. Evil, sin, and guilt are regarded as misperceptions. Sin is perceived as lack of love, or as a mistake calling for correction and love, rather than for guilt and punishment.

A Course In Miracles resonated with me with the same impact of Ken Keyes, because it asked that I be open to learning about love and higher consciousness.

Amidst this, I met a woman named Vicky, who was visiting from Arizona to facilitate support groups in studying and understanding of *A Course In Miracles*.

Only a few years older than me, she was so interesting, and reminded me of my dearest friends back at Cornucopia. I missed the intellectual exchange of ideas and insight I once had with my

Cornucopia family. Now, listening and learning from Vicky, I could have stayed all night because I loved what I was hearing and was hungry for more. As a result, I joined the weekly support group to study and participate in the daily lessons that *A Course in Miracles* offered. I wanted to continue drinking from the cup of knowledge and understanding.

Vicky and I became close friends. We communicated ideas freely and easily, and we understood each other on a spiritual level. I started to feel alive again.

I was beginning to be happy to see life anew. I started to sing and play my guitar, which I hadn't played since leaving the convent. I put the daily lessons from *A Course In Miracles* to music, and we sang them each time we met. It was a wondrous time, full of new ideas and growth.

While my mother remained in the ICU, I was able to see hope that my life was changing. I was beginning to remember again. I felt called. I began to remember how wonderful life can be when walking a spiritual path.

Vicky was going to return to Arizona after a three-month stay in Michigan.

"Do you want to come with me on the road across country to Unity Churches to help me facilitate and provide classes in *A Course In Miracles*?" she asked.

I was beside myself! I couldn't think of anything I would love more. Then reality hit me right in my heart.

Yet, how could I leave my mother? Doctors said she could exist in the ICU for several months or more.

"I understand why you can't leave," Vicky said. "If things change, I would love for you to catch up with me. My offer is always open."

When I returned to my father's house, I wanted to leave, but thinking about my mother kept me there. What would my family think if I left? They wouldn't understand, but I didn't understand why I allowed myself to stay and feel trapped. It didn't seem fair, but then, what is fair? Life sometimes is not fair.

One day, my father came home from the hospital all smiles. "Your mother is doing so much better," he said.

I knew he was lying. I had just seen her and she was not better. Then he started hugging me and trying to kiss me on the lips. He tried to put his tongue in my mouth.

I pushed him away and ran out of the house. I cried and cried.

Why did he do that?

No, I didn't want to know and I never wanted to remember, so I put the memory of that day with all the others away from my conscious mind, never to be remembered again, hidden, and safe from feeling.

That night, I slept outside in my car with the stars and moon keeping me company. After my father left for the hospital, I went back to the house to pack my things.

"I'm going to Arizona with you," I told Vicky by phone. "Can I stay with you until we leave?"

I told her I couldn't stay at my parents' place, though I didn't tell her why. I always felt like it was my fault somehow.

I left my father a note telling him I was leaving. I wrote, "I think you'll understand why."

I went to the hospital to say goodbye to my mother. It was and still is to this day the hardest thing, the most selfish thing I've ever done. My mother didn't understand how I could leave her when she was dying, but I had to leave. I couldn't stay another moment with my father. I thought if I did, I would die.

I said my goodbyes to my mother; my heart broken. I cried and cried. My heart and soul prayed for forgiveness and that she would someday understand. I was so confused by so many feelings not yet known to me. I wanted to stay, but I had to leave.

My mother lived for another three months in ICU. I was on my way back to Michigan when my brother called to say she passed. I was so hoping to see her one last time, but that night in a dream, she had told me: "I can't wait. They're calling me home."

She was finally at peace.

I actually knew she had passed before I got the call. She came to me in the still voice within my soul, saying: "I understand everything now. I'm happy and well. You need to do the same."

Despite that, I still haven't forgiven myself for leaving her. Maybe someday I will.

After the funeral, I returned to Arizona and continued my journey. Life was improving, and I was feeling more at peace with my mother's passing.

However, it seemed like no matter what, something would trigger a feeling in me, and I would start to feel that old torment in my soul. The dark feelings always came back to haunt me like an unwanted dream, bringing up feelings and fears that didn't make sense.

Meanwhile, Vicky and I made our way around to different Unity Churches, talking and sharing *A Course In Miracles*. It was one of the happiest times in my life. I was writing songs again and singing. I was happy!

During our travels, we came across another teacher called Ramtha, a spiritual entity who lived 35,000 years ago. In order to hear his teachings, we went to California for the fascinating experience of hearing an American New Age teacher named J. Z. Knight channel Ramtha to share his messages.

Ramtha's teachings were enlightening. He spoke to a knowing place within me... that place in my heart where I knew truth lived. His teachings aroused such joy and feelings of universal love! While following Ramtha's teachings, I met a man at one of the weekend retreats. I was certain that God had sent him to me. He was a captain in the Air Force, also on a spiritual path. I was attracted to him, and he was attracted to me.

Wow, finally!

After a long and thorough interrogation that any good social worker would conduct before dating someone, he assured me that he had never been married nor did he have any children. It would have been fine if he were divorced for at least a year or more, and I would have loved if he had children. To make a long story short, we dated for about a year with him traveling most weekends from his home in Virginia to visit me in Arizona.

Meanwhile, Vicky and I eventually discontinued our journey and continued on other paths, always remaining friends.

Don and I got engaged, and decided to live together, so I moved to Virginia. I hoped this would confirm our compatibility and that we were supposed to be together. Unfortunately, after living with Don for two months, I got a call from his wife.

He had lied about everything!

I left the next day.

Here again, life was providing yet another painful lesson. That's when I vowed:

I promise myself to give up on relationships. Sexual ones at least.

Chapter 14

HERE'S ANOTHER LIFE-CHANGING STORY that happened while my mother was still living. I became very ill with stomach pains and nausea so severe, I stayed in bed holding my stomach for many days.

I prayed that either the pain would stop or that I would die. I finally went to the doctor, and after many tests, he wanted to do exploratory surgery because he suspected that a tumor was growing on my pancreas.

If cancer had been discovered, I would have died. Fortunately, I am here to tell the story. The doctor found a tumor. However, it was at the tail end of my pancreas, and it was not cancerous. Removing that portion of my pancreas caused me to become a diabetic, and I remain so today. After surgery, I was in a coma for three days. I don't remember the coma, except for the stories that my mother shared.

Then I watched a special on TV featuring Elizabeth Kubler-Ross. She was a Swiss-American psychiatrist, a pioneer in near-death studies and the author of the groundbreaking book *On Death and Dying*, in which she first discussed her theory of the five stages of grief. Elizabeth Kubler-Ross also shared many of her patients' near-death experiences. That's when I started to remember mine: I saw my very thin body lying on the operating table. I hovered above, watching with such curiosity and interest as the doctors operated on me. I found myself traveling higher and higher to the brightest light I've ever seen, to a place of such profound joy and unconditional love. I did not see bodies, but I felt light beings all around me, so accepting, so loving beyond anything I've ever experienced here on earth. I went to the land beyond where all that exists is Divine Love. I felt the love of God all around me. I did not want to return. As soon as I thought the word "return," I was back in my body, back in my hospital room. My parents were at my bedside looking sad. I wanted to tell them I was back, not to worry, and that I would be awake soon.

I remember what everyone was wearing, what they said to each other, and what the doctor told them as I hovered above them. I will never forget my experience, and thus I have no fear of crossing over into the Oneness of God.

After that TV show and remembering my own near-death experience, I had the opportunity to study two summers with the late Elizabeth Kubler-Ross in Escondido, California. She only liked to be called Elizabeth, never Liz or Beth. That was a no-no.

I learned so much those summers; I grew to understand that death is nothing to fear and that it's all part of our wonderful journey. Elizabeth taught that it was important to heal any unfinished business or unresolved issues before crossing over so as not to take them with us to the other side.

I remember one workshop I attended that helped us get in touch with our unresolved issues. Elizabeth suggested we hit a pillow as hard as we could with a plastic baseball bat. She said the hitting of the bat would bring to the surface some of those unresolved issues. The bat hitting the pillow made such a horrendous, frightening, and for me a horrifying sound. It did, indeed, bring up feelings in me that I wasn't sure I liked or that I wanted to explore.

When it was my turn to hit the pillow, out of nowhere I found myself swinging the bat and striking the pillow with such force and passion. The intensity must have come from something inside me that needed to be released. Something was being brought to the surface. Something from my past. My unresolved issues. I felt emotions beyond words. Pain, fear, terror, and panic overwhelmed me. I saw and felt things from my past that left me unresponsive, unable to speak, as if in a shadow of death.

After hitting and hitting the pillow, I fell to the floor sobbing. It was a cry so deep, a cry so profoundly forbidden, that I lay alone with my memories that I had kept hidden, never wanting to awaken them. I just lay there on the cold, forsaken floor, not wanting anyone to touch or assist me in any way; I wanted to be alone, I wanted to get back to the land of forgetting.

I don't remember much of the following day, and no one brought up what they witnessed the day before. I do think that sometimes when such raw emotions are exposed, people usually don't want to bring it up again. So I locked up those feelings of that day as yet another bad dream. I put the memories of that day in the place where such knowledge and feelings need to remain, never allowing them to surface again.

I continued working and studying with Elizabeth, and I will be forever grateful for her courage and strength to talk about such personal issues of death and dying. I also had the opportunity to study with her and Gregg M. Furth, author of *The Secret World of Drawings: A Jungian Approach to Healing Through Art*.

Remembering and Forgetting

I was trained on how to interpret and understand what others are feeling — and sometimes what they are hiding — through what they draw. It is very rewarding and insightful. I have used this technique in working with children who didn't have the language to assist them in expressing their feelings. Children always seem to be willing to draw when given the chance and to share what they just drew. I would ask them to draw me three pictures: The first: of them and their family doing something together when they were five years old. The second: one of their family now. The third drawing could be anything they wanted to draw. I was always impressed with the wonderful pictures being presented to me with colors that expressed such deep emotions and the story being told in the form of art. The children were always eager to share their stories, their rainbows, stars, homes, family, and pets. I was always drawn into their experiences and felt it a privilege that they shared so openly with me.

Chapter 15

When I returned to Michigan, where I live now, I still had the feeling that I had been sleepwalking through life, not knowing where I was going or how I was feeling. I was merely existing.

I just got up every day, went to work, did my best, and masked my pain. I laughed, I cried, I joked around like always. I had wonderful friends, but I was not awake, not really.

I knew from reading self-help books and studying that every one of us needs to look inside ourselves and love who we are, not look outside in search of love or acceptance. I loved the concept, and I believed it, yet I didn't think it could be true for me. I came to realize that I didn't like the person inside of me. I had too much hidden, too many memories to keep buried, too many stories that no one would believe.

Instead, I had been living in the shadow of all those I had come to admire and love, believing that their lives were so much richer and more alive than mine, so all my happiness, sorrow, joy, and adventures were theirs.

With each new relationship, life was wonderful, full of new adventures, friends, and family. As a child, I always wanted my friends' families to be mine, and I would pretend they were. I would daydream, thinking that somehow living in my friend's house with her loving parents would be so wonderful — without the anger, sadness, or craziness that I experienced in mine.

I kept doing that in adulthood, always thinking someone else's life would be better, fuller, happier. As each relationship ended, I blamed myself, thinking if I were just a little more understanding, more loving, more of what the other person needed me to be, the relationship would have thrived. Then I, too, would be happier, but no, I would find another relationship with another person's life to live, only to be disappointed in the end. As hard as I tried to be what I thought the other person needed, what I thought they wanted, it always ended the same. I found out who they were, but not who I was.

The longest and probably the most fulfilled relationship brought extreme highs and lows and lasted more than 22 years. I experienced the depth and sorrow of death and the miracle of birth. I was able — if only in my fantasies — to experience a little of what having a family of my own would be like. I always wanted to be part of a family and have a family of my own. I ached for that make-believe family that celebrated holidays and birthdays and did things together during the good times and the bad.

The platonic relationship felt safe. For the first time, I felt I had a family. I lived this fantasy all these years thinking my friend's family was mine. They were great years with many wonderful, joyful memories — along with some of the most painful ones. My beloved friend asked me not to write about her in my book, so I will honor that. However, I will share my own life experiences and journey these past years.

My beloved friend's relatives, grandchildren, and friends became mine. It wasn't fair to her or me, but I didn't know at the time how this type of attachment could put a strain on a friendship.

a spirtual journey

During this relationship, my father passed away. I still don't know how I feel about it, but I made sure I didn't make the same mistake as with my mother's passing. Instead, I did whatever I could to assist in my father's care, except I knew he could never live with me. I took him to some of his doctor's appointments and his dialysis appointments whenever I could. And I tried to do whatever else my family asked of me, albeit with a disturbed heart.

I was not with my father when he passed, but the day before he died, I took the day off from work and sat by his bedside. He was taken off his dialysis and only had a few days to live, if that.

When I sat next to him, he appeared so helpless, unable to speak due to his body letting go of life to cross over to the other side. He looked so old — like a skeleton of his old self. And for the first time, I was not afraid to be alone with him. I wanted so much to feel something. But all of my feelings for my father were in that secret place that I kept hidden, even from myself.

As I sought love and belonging in my relationship with my special friend, I talked her into allowing me to get a dog. I had to beg and plead, stating I didn't have anything to call my own. So after several months, I was finally able to get my puppy. Abbie, my little Yorkie, was the joy of my life, perhaps the joy of having a living, breathing, warm and loving little dog that loved me. I know some people may find this strange, but it was wonderful knowing that when I came home from work, Abbie would be so excited, running around the house, her tail wagging, jumping into my arms as I bent down to hug her.

Abbie was the closest I ever came to a having a child. She was dependent on me for life, and I was dependent on her. I never liked leaving her, and I know she didn't like that I left her. We did everything together. She slept with me every night and cuddled next to me with her little warm body. I had Abbie in my life just shy of one week of her tenth birthday; she died of liver cancer. Her death was a profound loss; I didn't think my heart could hurt to that depth of sorrow and pain. I didn't know what to do with myself. I walked around in a fog, and I cried like a mother who lost their child. I couldn't sleep without her next to me, so I took her baby blanket and held it close to me so I could smell her scent on the blanket and see her tiny hairs left behind. These feeling lasted for several months. I miss her every day, but I also know I was blessed to have her in my life. I believe all animals that we humans come to love are like little angels that arrive to teach us about unconditional love.

I continued to worked as a social worker/case manager at a community mental health agency. I worked with mentally ill and developmentally disabled adults and children. I loved my job, the clients, and their families. My co-workers were the best. I call many of them friends and we meet monthly for lunch.

I retired two years ago. It was time. I was getting burned out with all the bureaucracy of a county job. It was difficult retiring, only because I was fully aware that my work life was ending. That chapter of my life was over. I had no plans or thoughts of what I would do after retirement.

When I retired, I was in bad shape, suffering from a variety of medical and physical issues. I weighed 252 pounds. I had severe arthritis in both knees, my back, and my neck. I was in constant pain. I was diagnosed with fibromyalgia, sleep apnea, high blood pressure, high cholesterol, and insulin-dependent diabetes. I had a total knee replacement, and two years later needed a revision replacement surgery. I was unable to walk without a cane and required a scooter if I needed to walk for any long distance. All I wanted to do was sleep. I had no energy. I couldn't, nor did I want to go anywhere. I was convinced I had some awful illness like cancer and was going to die. I tried to put on a good face to hide my pain.

This time of extreme suffering propelled me back onto my spiritual path. Many times in my life, I would be spiritually alive until life became too busy, and I would get too involved in everyday living. Then my spirituality would be forgotten.

Thus, the name of the book is *Remembering and Forgetting*. I would forget how wonderful I felt, how much more alive I was when listening and being aware that there is something much bigger than myself. I had always prayed every day of my life, but most of the time it was out of habit. I don't even remember how it started, but I found myself meditating and developing a more authentic relationship with God, my angels, and guides again. I was beginning to pray with a sincere heart and a desire to become whole again… as I once had, perhaps years ago when I was in the convent.

One of my best friends from work, Debbie, and I were always going on diets that included signing up for Weight Watchers and Medical Weight Loss Clinic.

After I retired, Debbie and I were talking on the phone when I said, "Let's go back to Weight Watchers."

"No," we agreed. "We both just kept giving them money and are never able to stay on it."

"Maybe you should go to a hypnotist for weight loss," Debbie suggested. "If it works for you, I'll do it, too."

I Googled hypnotists in my area and called about three. Two of them gave me a bad feeling. I liked the third one because I could meet in person for only $25.

Chapter 16

MY LIFE TOTALLY CHANGED on September 27, 2017, when I had an appointment to meet with Dr. Kim Manning, a hypnotherapist. Her office was in the higher rent district of Oakland County in a very professional-looking building. My first thought was, *I am not going to be able to afford her services.* I didn't think hypnotherapy would work for me, anyway. I just thought I would give it a try. I needed to lose weight, and had tried everything else. I was impressed with her title: Kim Manning, PhD, Certified Medical Hypnotherapist. I also really liked the name of her business: Focused Solutions Hypnotherapy.

Wow, what an elaborate and well-decorated office, I thought, *and this is just the waiting room.* Within seconds, the main office door opened and there stood a petite, attractive, brown-haired, well-dressed woman with kind eyes and an engaging smile. She introduced herself and asked me to fill out some paperwork. She said to just come into her office when I was finished. When I completed the paperwork, I timidly walked into her office. It was beautifully and professionally decorated in a simple but elegant style. Dr. Manning offered me a seat to the side of her desk. The office felt warm and inviting, putting me at ease as Dr. Manning looked over my paperwork.

With her radiant smile and kind eyes, Dr. Manning spoke in a soft, caring voice.

"What do you think I can help you with?" she asked.

"I want to lose weight," I said.

"Tell me about your diet history."

"I've been on every diet out there," I said. "I'll lose some weight, then gain it back with even more."

Then Dr. Manning told me the most outrageous and shocking thing I have ever heard: "It's obvious that diets don't work for you, and you should never diet again."

Never diet again? Was she out of her mind? How can I lose weight without dieting?

Then Dr. Manning suggested that I not use the word "lose," because my subconscious mind would go looking for the weight I lost. She suggested I use the word "release." It took me a long time to remember to use the word release instead of lose, but I rarely forget now.

"I'm on a spiritual path, and I believe in angels and spiritual beings," I said. "I'm a spiritual person, not a religious person. I believe I'm being guided to live a more meaningful and complete life."

I told her about my guardian angel named Myrtle and Archangel Raphael who watched over me, and that I communicated daily with them in prayer and meditation. I considered them spiritual friends. I told her these things in hopes she wouldn't think I was "mental." I needed her to understand the path I was on, and if she felt comfortable or had a problem with it, I needed to know. Dr. Manning said she felt comfortable with what I shared. She also felt she could help me with my weight issues.

It was a no-brainer for me to sign up for my first five sessions. Her services were affordable and not outrageous as I had feared. I felt very comfortable, believing I needed to give this hypnosis thing a chance. I've been meeting with Dr. Manning ever since.

My first hypnosis session was a little unnerving because I didn't know what to expect, even though Dr. Manning had explained some of it during the interview session.

Here's what happened.

I sat next to her desk.

"How are you feeling?" she asked, standing up. "It's time to begin. Please remove your shoes."

Oh, my God, I thought. *I hope my socks don't have a hole in them and that my feet don't smell!*

After taking off my shoes — relieved that I didn't have any holes in my socks — she invited me to sit in a leather loveseat recliner. The chair felt so comfortable as I sat down. Dr. Manning adjusted it to maximum recline, so I was lying completely flat. She covered me with a very soft fleece blanket; I later called it my protective shield. Dr. Manning gave me an eye mask to cover my eyes and to become as comfortable and relaxed as possible.

I was not afraid. She began the first, and every subsequent session, using her warm, gentle hypnotic voice, by saying: "And so, you can begin by taking in a nice, deep, full breath, and as you slowly let that breath go, just think the word 'relax,' and you can relax. Just relaxing in your own way, at your own pace, as little or as much as you choose. So whenever we work together, Lin, you are always in control, so realize you are safe in every way."

I can't tell you how comforting and reassuring those words were. I fell into her hypnotic spell knowing I was safe. Dr. Manning continued to say things like: "If you find your mind wandering as it sometimes will, just focus your attention to the tip of your nose and once again you will follow my voice. My voice is soothing to you and helps you to relax."

Dr. Manning also ended each session with: " ...and now it's time to bring the session to a close. In a moment, I'm going to count from one to five, and on the count of five, you'll return to full conscious awareness, normal wakeful alertness, feeling calm, focused, and centered. One: coming up slowly. Two: mind-body emotions completely under your control. Three: bringing all the suggestions with you that are for you or your benefit. Four: releasing anything that's not. Then on the next count: eyes open fully aware, alert, and awake."

When my session was over and I was slowly returning to the room, fully alert, I felt such a comforting, warm feeling, like Dr. Manning cared and wanted to help me. That thought somehow brought a sense of hope that maybe, just maybe, I would start to feel better, to release some weight. (Dr. Manning would be proud I remembered to say "release" instead of "lose" weight).

Today, I meet with Dr. Manning weekly.

All of my sessions have been profound and insightful, healing and rewarding, but not always pleasant. Dr. Manning escorted me to my hidden secret places, feelings, and experiences that I never wanted to visit again. She gently guided me. She accompanied me to my inner world, asking questions that needed asking. Some I was able to answer, some were just too painful, or I didn't have the words, just feelings. Dr. Manning seemed to hold my hands during these times without ever touching them. Her voice conveyed concern and understanding, never judgment. She seemed to know just how far to explore an issue and when to allow me to recover from painful remembrances. I called these sessions "going down the Rabbit Hole." Please note that Dr. Manning herself never used that term; I just called it that.

The Rabbit Hole was symbolic of my dark, secret, hidden fears lying deep within me where the root causes of my fears lived. I sometimes asked Dr. Manning if she was going to be taking me down the Rabbit Hole when I would come in for another session. She always seemed to know somehow when I was emotionally ready to go to those deep hidden places of my childhood and when I was not. Dr. Manning knew when I needed to recover from those memories hidden deeply in my subconscious mind to heal and reawaken to a more enlightened understanding.

One of my journeys down the Rabbit Hole is somewhat of a blur, but I will do my best to recall it. Then, as now, Dr. Manning manifested wisdom beyond anyone I have ever worked with, personally or professionally. I must admit that when I return to this journey, I am profoundly awed by my experience with her.

Allow me to take you on my journey: Dr. Manning escorted me to the recliner as she always did, placing the soft fleece blanket over me, my protective shield, and an eye mask on my face. Dr. Manning explained that she uses the eye mask "to defuse external distractions for a better internal focus."

Then she said, "I'm going to take you on a journey, and I will be guiding you. I want you to answer out loud."

I lay there shaking uncontrollably, knowing she would take me deeper and deeper into my subconscious mind, to that place I experienced a long time ago, but never wanted to return.

"What are you aware of?" she asked with her gentle voice. After a seemingly long silence, she asked, "What is happening there? Speak to me out loud."

I was mute, trapped in the memory, hovering over the scene of my past. I felt every emotion. I felt the pain. I saw the act ever so clearly in my mind's eye. It was terrifying, seeing and re-experiencing my childhood trauma. I felt catatonic, unable to move or speak, lost deep down in the Rabbit Hole.

Dr. Manning's voice sounded as if she were in a distant land. I wanted to speak, and I wanted her help, yet I felt like I was suffocating, being buried in that Rabbit Hole. I sensed her hand trying to pull me out, but no words or sounds came from me, as if a hand covered my mouth.

"Will you give me permission to speak to Archangel Raphael and your guardian angel Myrtle?" Dr. Manning asked.

"Yes," I said without hesitation. (Please note that as I am writing this, my heart is full of gratitude and tears fill my eyes).

"Archangel Raphael and Guardian Angel Myrtle, would you be willing to speak for Lin?" Dr. Manning asked.

"Yes," I answered, then began telling Dr. Manning what I was seeing and experiencing. I will forever be grateful for the wisdom and the divine guidance that Dr. Manning manifested that day in knowing just what to do and say to assist me in sharing that deeply hidden secret.

It took several weekly sessions for me to discover, with the help of Dr. Manning, that my childhood beliefs and experiences held me back, and that my weight issues were from me stuffing down feelings. The weight began to "release" without any effort on my part once I started letting go of my hidden fears. I was able to eat anything I wanted as long as I ate until I was satisfied, not full.

"If you eat until you are full," Dr. Manning explained, "then you are overeating. Put small bites in your mouth and chew your food completely."

I did everything Dr. Manning suggested and listened to the weekly CDs she sent home with me, at least two or more times a day.

I truly believe Dr. Manning is a miracle worker. My physical health greatly improved, and I was able to walk without a cane and for long distances without any pain. I didn't need my sleep apnea machine anymore, and all other health issues greatly improved. I was not tired anymore; I haven't taken a nap in months. I feel fully alive and awake, full of energy, love, and hope for a future without illness or fear.

I did have a little setback: I was diagnosed with breast cancer during the Christmas 2017 season. I believe that I created that when I feared that I was going to die. I kept thinking I was dying and that I probably had cancer. I've learned a little of how the subconscious mind works from Dr. Manning, and all my subconscious mind kept hearing was the word cancer, and thus I got cancer. I was truly blessed however because the breast cancer diagnosis was at stage one, level one.

I had my surgery to remove the cancerous tumor on January 5, 2018. Dr. Manning made me a beautiful healing CD to hear while in surgery. The CD took me on a journey to a place of healing energy and love. I felt an intense feeling of deep affection, tenderness, and warmth. I felt as though I was being surrounded and cradled in the softness of divine love. Dr. Manning asked God, my angels, and guides to assist in the operating room guiding my surgeon's hand while removing the cancerous tumor. The CD powerfully guided me to the road of healing recovering. No cancer was found in my lymph nodes, so all I needed was radiation treatment and a pill I need to take for the next five years to block any cancer from entering my cells.

Without the healing experiences of hypnotherapy and the professional wisdom of Dr. Manning, I truly believe I wouldn't be here today. I would have created the end of my life experience. I now know that I had to die to live again. Some people call it a rebirth experience. I call it an awakening to all that is; being able to face my fears and to be willing to go down the Rabbit Hole, into the darkness, and then into the light. It has been an experience that I feel so blessed and thankful for, to be aware that without the support and guidance of Dr. Manning, Archangel Raphael, Guardian Angel Myrtle, and all my other angels, saints, and guides I wouldn't have remembered… I would have remained lost in forgetting. Now I celebrate my life of *Remembering and Forgetting*.

I have been so blessed! With the assistance of my spiritual support team, lovingly guiding me and with the gentle reassurance from Dr. Manning I can and will become whole again in body, mind, and spirit. And by my willingness to go to those deep, hidden places where fear and shame lived only to experience that there was nothing to fear after all. I walked into the light and saw myself cradled in the arms of a loving God with all His healing love and acceptance.

To those in my life today, family and friends, knowingly or unknowingly, I felt your love and support. I have come to realize that I once knew things, but now I *know* things. I know that God in His Divine wisdom and love, and acceptance of every one of us, He only asks that we believe that there is nothing to fear, that only love exists.

Epilogue

A *Thank You* for Dr. Kim Manning.

How do you thank someone who introduced you to the experience of hypnosis in finding the focused solutions to reach your authentic self?

How do you thank someone who's opened the door to your subconscious mind using an hypnotic voice only found in celestial realms, allowing healing to occur without your even knowing?

How do you thank someone who blankets you with the warmth and softness of a protective shield as you dare to wake the fearful child within?

How do you thank someone who believes in magic, who introduces you to "creatures who live in the silent depths of the sea and invites you to swim in a silken sea of golden mist in a distant planet"?

How do you thank someone who holds your hand without ever touching it as you venture into unknown places?

How do you thank someone who believes in you, before you do, by encouraging and reinforcing that you can accomplish anything you want?

How do you thank someone who knows when to soothe your uncontrollably beating heart that's fearful to speak the unknown lying just below the surface and gently taking you on a more calm and peaceful inner journey of discovering?

How do you thank someone who appears to be accompanied by angels and guides and speaks of healing and taking risks?

How do you thank someone who helps you find the courage and strength to take the necessary steps to reach your desired goals?

How do you thank someone who says, "That's right," or "Very good" at just the right time?

How do you thank someone who's given birth to all that you were meant to be; who saw the good and sincerity of your soul; and who saw the God within?

So, how do you *thank* someone?

You just do!

I want to thank you, Dr. Kim Manning, for your genuine support and encouragement for me to become my fully, healthy and fit self.

In gratitude, Lin

About Lin Day

LIN DAY HAS 44 years of professional experience in Psychology and Human Development. She has aided people of all ages, deepening her understanding of how to help others move beyond their own self-imposed limitations.

Lin is a certified bereavement and grief counselor, having studied death and dying with Elizabeth Kubler-Ross as well as interpretation of art with Gregg M. Furth in Escondido, California. Lin lived at Cornucopia in Kentucky and studied with Ken Keyes, author of several books, including his *Handbook to Higher Consciousness*.

Lin spent several years working with individuals suffering from chronic and persistent mental illness in psychiatric hospitals. and in the past 18 years worked for Macomb County Mental Health as a Case Manager/Social Worker. Her compassion for life is expressed in her love of all people and their growth. Lin was often heard saying, "When a client of mine is successful so am I."

The Macomb County Community Mental Health Board stated: "For 18 years, Lin Day, has with a mix of good humor and passion, championed the interest and dignity of adults and children with mental illness and developmental disabilities who are served by MCCMH as a case manager."

Lin loves music and has been known to write and sing many of her own affirmations on her guitar. Lin meditates and prays daily, as both are very important to her.

Lin is a lover of nature, all of God's children, animals, and all that life has to offer. She hopes this book may be helpful somehow!

www.ingramcontent.com/pod-product-compliance
Lightning Source LLC
Chambersburg PA
CBHW021156080526
44588CB00008B/371